I0022568

Golfing Society Edinburgh Burgess

Poems on Golf

Golfing Society Edinburgh Burgess

Poems on Golf

ISBN/EAN: 9783337005634

Printed in Europe, USA, Canada, Australia, Japan

Cover: Foto ©Thomas Meinert / pixelio.de

More available books at **www.hansebooks.com**

SOME Members of THE EDINBURGH BURGESS
GOLFING SOCIETY having resolved to collect and
print a few fugitive pieces in verse relating to the
game of GOLF, the following Poems and Songs
have been after some labour procured, and are
now printed (some for the first time) for private
circulation among the Subscribers whose names
are appended.

EDINBURGH, *April* 1867.

CONTENTS.

✦

LIST OF SUBSCRIBERS.

✦

BANNATYNE, ADAM B., Advocate.

BARCLAY, JAS., Writer.

BAYLEY, GEO., W.S.

BELL, W. H., A.C.S.

BEVERIDGE, WILL. T. R., A.C.S.

BRODIE, WM., R.S.A.

BROWN, W. A., Advocate.

BROWN, THOMAS, Writer.

BURN, GEORGE, W.S.

CALDER, A., Insurance Manager.

CHISHOLM, JOHN K., Dentist.

CLARK, AND. R., Advocate.

CLARK, R., Printer.

CURROR, D., S.S.C.

DRUMMOND, JAMES, R.S.A.

DRYSDALE WILLIAM, D.C.S.

FRASER. WM. N., of Tornaveen.

GOUGH, OWEN, Holyrood Palace.

HAY, JAMES, Esq., Leith.

HENDERSON, ANDREW, Writer.

HENDERSON, DAVID, Writer.

HUTCHISON, II., Writer.

HUTTON, WM., Writer.

JACK, JNO., Writer.

JAMIESON, JAMES T., S.S.C.

JOHNSTON, ROB., Solicitor.

KINNEAR, JAS., Writer.

KIRKWOOD, JAMES, Merchant.

LANDALE, THO., S.S.C.

LEE, ROBERT, Advocate.

LEGGAT, JAMES, Coal Master.

LEISHMAN, JOHN, W.S.

MACKENZIE, JOHN, W.S.

MACMILLAN, II., Writer.

M'EWEN, J., Writer.

MANN, W., Writer.

MELVILLE, F. SUTHER, A.C.S.

MILLAR, WM., Board of Supervision.

MITCHELL, A., Banker.

MONCREIFF, JAMES, M.P., Dean
of the Faculty of Advocates.

MONCRIEFF, A., Advocate.

MORRISON, AD., S.S.C.

MURRAY, ANDW., Jun., W.S.

PATTISON, G. H., Advocate.

REID, WILLIAM, Writer.

SHAW, ROBERT B., Assistant Clerk of the Bills

SMITH, DANIEL, Corn Factor.

STEVEN, ROBERT, Writer.

STEVENSON, PETER, Philosophical Instrument
Maker.

THOMS, GEO. H., Advocate.

THOMPSON, J. GIBSON.

THOMSON, JOHN, S.S.C.

THOMSON, W. M., Advocate.

WADDELL, ALEX. PEDDIE, W.S.

WELCH, C., Writer, Cupar.

WILLIAMSON, JAMES, Traveller.

WILSON, GEO. B., Accountant.

YOUNG, J. WM., 22 Royal Circus.

THE GOFF.

By THOMAS MATHISON, originally a Writer in Edinburgh, and afterwards Minister of Brechin. Reprinted from the second edition of the Poem. 1763.

CANTO I.

GOFF, and the *Man*, I sing, who, em'lous, plies
  The jointed club, whose balls invade the skies,
Who from *Edina's* tow'rs, his peaceful home,
In quest of fame o'er *Letha's* plains did roam.
Long toil'd the hero, on the verdant field,
Strain'd his stout arm the weighty club to wield:
Such toils it cost, such labours to obtain
The bays of conquest, and the bowl to gain.
  O thou GOLFINIA, Goddess of these plains !
Great Patroness of GOFF ! indulge my strains :
Whether beneath the *thorn-tree* shade you lie,
Or from *Mercerian* tow'rs the game survey.

Or round the green the flying ball you chase,

Or make your bed in some hot sandy *face :*

Leave your much-lov'd abode, inspire his lays

Who sings of GOFF, and sings thy fav'rite's praise.

North from *Edina* eight furlongs and more,

Lies that fam'd field, on *Fortha's* sounding shore.

Here *Caledonian* Chiefs for health resort,

Confirm their sinews by the manly sport.

Macdonald and unmatch'd *Dalrymple* ply

Their pond'rous weapons, and the green defy :

Rattray for skill, and *Corse* for strength renown'd,

Stewart and *Lesly* beat the sandy ground,

And *Brown* and *Alston,* Chiefs well known to fame,

And numbers more the Muse forbears to name.

Gigantic *Biggar* here full oft is seen,

Like huge behemoth on an *Indian* green ;

His bulk enormous scarce can 'scape the eyes,

Amaz'd spectators wonder how he plies.

Yea, here great *Forbes,** patron of the just,

The dread of villains and the good man's trust,

Duncan Forbes, Lord President of the Court of Session in Scotland.

When spent with toils in serving human kind,

His body recreates, and unbends his mind.

    Bright *Phœbus* now had measur'd half the day,

And warm'd the earth with genial noon-tide ray :

Forth rush'd *Castalio* and his daring foe,

Both arm'd with clubs, and eager for the blow.

Of finest ash Castalio's shaft was made,

Pond'rous with lead, and fenc'd with horn the head

(The work of *Dickson*, who in *Letha* dwells,

And in the art of making clubs excels),

Which late beneath great *Claro's* arm did bend,

But now is wielded by his greater friend.

    Not with more fury *Norris* cleav'd the main,

To pour his thund'ring arms on guilty *Spain ;*

Nor with more haste brave *Haddock* bent his course

To guard *Minorca* from *Iberian* force,—

Than thou, intrepid hero, urg'd thy way

O'er roads and sands, impatient for the fray.

    With equal warmth *Pygmalion* fast pursu'd

(With courage oft are little wights endued).

"Till to GOLFINIA's downs the heroes came,

The scene of combat and the field of fame.

Upon a verdant bank by *Flora* grac'd,

Two sister Fairies found the Goddess plac'd :

Propp'd by her snowy hand her head reclin'd.

Her curling locks hung waving in the wind.

She eyes intent the consecrated green,

Crowded with waving clubs and vot'ries keen,

And hears the prayers of youths to her address'd,

And from the hollow face relieves the ball distress'd.

On either side the sprightly Dryads sat,

And entertained the Goddess with their chat.

First VERDURILLA, thus : O rural Queen !

What chiefs are those that drive along the green !

With brandish'd clubs the mighty heroes threat,

Their eager looks foretell a keen debate.

To whom GOLFINIA : Nymph, your eyes behold

Pygmalion stout, *Castalio* brave and bold.

From silver *Ierna's* banks *Castalio* came,

But first on *Andrean* plains he courted fame.

His sire, a Druid, taught (one day of seven)

The paths of virtue, the sure road to heaven.

In *Pictish* capital the good man passed

His virtuous life, and there he breath'd his last.

The son now dwells in fair *Edina's* town.

And on our sandy plains pursues renown.

See low *Pygmalion*, skilled in GOFFING art,

Small is his size, but dauntless is his heart :

Fast by a desk in *Edin's* domes he sits,

With *saids* and *sicklikes* length'ning out the writs.

For no mean prize the rival chiefs contend,

But full rewards the victor's toils attend.

The vanquish'd hero for the victor fills

A mighty bowl containing thirty gills :

With noblest liquor is the bowl replete ;

Here sweets and acids, strength and weakness meet.

From *Indian* isles the strength and sweetness flow.

And *Tagus'* banks their golden fruits bestow :

Cold *Caledonia's* lucid streams controul

The fiery spirits, and fulfil the bowl :

For *Albion's* peace and *Albion's* friends they pray.

And drown in *Punch* the labours of the day.

    The Goddess spoke, and thus GAMBOLIA pray'd :

Permit to join in brave *Pygmalion's* aid,

O'er each deep road the hero to sustain.

And guide his ball to the desired plain.

To this the Goddess of the manly sport :

Go, and be thou that daring chief's support.

Let VERDURILLA be *Castalio's* stay ;

I from this flow'ry seat will view the fray.

She said : the nymphs trip nimbly o'er the green.

And to the combatants approach unseen.

END OF CANTO I.

CANTO II.

Ye rural powers that on these plains preside,
Ye nymphs that dance on Fortha's flow'ry side,
Assist the Muse that in your fields delights,
And guide her course in these uncommon flights.
But chief, thee, O GOLFINIA ! I implore,
High as thy balls instruct my Muse to soar :
So may thy green for ever crowded be,
And balls on balls invade the azure sky.

    Now at that hole the chiefs begin the game,
Which from the neighb'ring *thorn-tree* takes its name :
Ardent they grasp the ball-compelling clubs,
And stretch their arms t' attack the little globes :
Not as our warriors brandish'd dreadful arms,
When fierce *Bellona* sounded war's alarms :
When conqu'ring *Cromwell* stain'd fair *Eska's* flood,
And soak'd her banks with *Caledonian* blood :

Or when our bold ancestors madly fought,

And clans engaged for trifles or for nought,

That *Fury* now from our bless'd fields is driv'n,

To scourge unhappy nations doom'd by heav'n.

Let *Kouli Kan* destroy the fertile East,

Victorious *Vernon* thunder in the West :

Let horrid war involve perfidious *Spain,*

And GEORGE assert his empire o'er the main :

But on our plains *Britannia's* sons engage,

And void of ire the sportive war they wage.

Lo, tatter'd *Irus,* who their armour bears,

Upon the green two little pyr'mids rears :

On these they place two balls with careful eye.

That with *Clarinda's* breasts for colour vie,—

The work of *Bobson,* who, with matchless art,

Shapes the firm hide, connecting ev'ry part.—

Then in a socket sets the well-stitched void,

And thro' the eyelet drives the downy tide :

Crowds urging crowds the forceful brogue impels,

The feathers harden and the leather swells :

He crams and sweats, yet crams and urges more,

Till scarce the turgid globe contains its store :

The dreadful falcon's pride here blended lies

With pigeons' glossy down of various dyes ;

The lark's small pinions join the common stock,

And yellow glory of the martial cock.

Soon as *Hyperion* gilds old *Andrea's* spires,

From bed the artist to his cell retires,

With bended back, there plies his steely awls,

And shapes, and stuffs, and finishes the balls.

But when the glorious God of day has driv'n

His flaming chariot down the steep of heav'n,

He ends his labour, and with rural strains

Enchants the lovely maids and weary swains :

As thro' the streets the blythsome piper plays,

In antic dance they answer to his lays ;

At ev'ry pause the ravish'd crowd acclaim,

And rends the skies with tuneful *Bobson's* name.

Not more rewarded was old *Amphion's* song,

That reared a town, and this drags one along.

Such is fam'd *Bobson*, who in *Andrea* thrives,

And such the balls each vig'rous hero drives.

First, bold *Castalio*, ere he struck the blow,

Lean'd on his club, and thus address'd his foe :

Dares weak *Pygmalion this* stout arm defy,

Which brave *Matthias* doth with terror try?

Strong as he is, *Moravio* owns my might,

Distrusts his vigour, and declines the fight.

Renown'd *Clephanio* I constrain'd to yield,

And drove the haughty vet'ran from the field.

Weak is thine arm, rash youth! thy courage vain;

Vanquish'd, with shame you'll curse the fatal plain.

The half-struck balls your weak endeavours mock,

Slowly proceed, and soon forget the stroke.

Not so the orb eludes my thund'ring force,

Thro' fields of air it holds its rapid course;

Swift as the balls from martial engines driv'n,

Streams like a comet thro' the arch of heav'n.

Vaunter, go on! (*Pygmalion* thus replies);

Thine empty boasts with justice I despise!

Hadst thou the strength Goliah's spear to wield,

Like its great master thunder on the field,

And with that strength *Culloden's* matchless art,

Not one unmanly thought should daunt my heart.

He said: and sign'd to *Irus*, who before

With frequent warnings fill'd the sounding shore.

Then great *Castalio* his whole strength collects,

And on the orb a noble blow directs ;

Swift as a thought the ball obedient flies,

Sings high in air, and seems to cleave the skies :

Then on the level plain its fury spends ;

And *Irus* to the chief the welcome tidings sends.

Next in his turn *Pygmalion* strikes the globe :

On the upper half descends the erring club ;

Along the green the ball confounded scours ;

No lofty flight the ill-sped stroke impow'rs.

Thus, when the trembling hare descries the hounds,

She from her whinny mansion swiftly bounds ;

O'er hills and fields she scours, outstrips the wind :

The hounds and huntsmen follow far behind.

Gambolia now afforded timely aid,

She o'er the sand the fainting ball convey'd ;

Renew'd its force, and urg'd it on its way,

Till on the summit of the hill it lay.

Now all on fire the chiefs their orbs pursue,

With the next stroke the orbs their flight renew ;

Thrice round the green they urge the whizzing ball.

And thrice three holes to great *Castalio* fall :

The other six *Pygmalion* bore away,
And saved a while the honours of the day.

　Had some brave champion of the sandy field
The chiefs attended, and the game beheld,
With ev'ry stroke his wonder had increas'd,
And em'lous fires had kindled in his breast.

 END OF CANTO II.

CANTO III.

HARMONIOUS Nine, that from *Parnassus* view
The subject world, and all that's done below ;
Who from oblivion snatch the patriot's name.
And to the stars extol the hero's fame :
Bring each your lyre, and to my song repair.
Nor think *Golfinia's* train below the Muses' care.

Declining *Sol* with milder beams invades
The *Scotian* fields, and lengthens out the shades :
Hastes to survey the conquer'd golden plains.
Where captive *Indians* mourn in *Spanish* chains,
To gild the waves where hapless *Hosier* dy'd,
Where *Vernon* late proud *Bourbon's* force defied.
Triumphant rode along the wat'ry plain,
Britannia's glory and the scourge of *Spain.*

Still from her seat the *Power* of GOFF beheld
Th' unwearied heroes toiling on the field :

The light-foot fairies in their labours share,

Each nymph her hero seconds in the war;

PYGMALION and *Gambolia* there appear,

And VERDURILLA with *Castalio* here.

The Goddess saw, and op'd the book of Fate.

To search the issue of the grand debate.

Bright silver plates the sacred leaves enfold,

Bound with twelve shining clasps of solid gold.

The wond'rous book contains the fate of all

That lift the club, and strike the missive ball ;

Mysterious rhymes, that thro' the pages flow,

The past, the present, and the future show.

GOLFINIA reads the fate-foretelling lines,

And soon the sequel of the war divines ;

Sees conquest doom'd *Castalio's* toils to crown.

Pygmalion doom'd superior might to own.

Then at her side VICTORIA straight appears,

Her sister goddess, arbitress of wars ;

Upon her head a wreath of bays she wore,

And in her hand a laurel sceptre bore ;

Anxious to know the will of Fate, she stands,

And waits obsequious on the Queen's commands.

To whom Golfinia : Fate-fulfilling maid,

Hear the Fates' will, and be their will obey'd :

Straight to the field of fight thyself convey,

Where brave *Castalio* and *Pygmalion* stray ;

There bid the long-protracted combat cease,

And with thy bays *Castalio's* temples grace.—

She said ; and swift, as *Hermes* from above

Shoots to perform the high behests of *Jove*,

Victoria from her sister's presence flies,

Pleased to bestow the long-disputed prize.

Meanwhile the chiefs for the last hole contend.

The last great hole, which should their labours end ;

For this the chiefs exert their skill and might.

To drive the balls, and to direct their flight.

Thus two fleet coursers for the Royal plate

(The others distanc'd) run the final heat ;

With all his might each gen'rous racer flies.

And all his art each panting rider tries,

While show'rs of gold and praises warm his breast,

And gen'rous emulation fires the beast.

His trusty club *Pygmalion* dauntless plies :

The ball ambitious climbs the lofty skies :

But soon, ah ! soon, descends upon the field,

The adverse winds the lab'ring orb repell'd.

Thus when a fowl, whom wand'ring sportsmen scare,

Leaves the sown land, and mounts the fields of air,

Short is his flight ; the fiery *Furies* wound,

And bring him tumbling headlong to the ground.

Not so *Castalio* lifts th' unerring club,

But with superior art attacks the globe ;

The well-struck ball the stormy wind beguil'd,

And like a swallow skimm'd along the field.

An harmless sheep, by Fate decreed to fall,

Feels the dire fury of the rapid ball ;

Full on her front the raging bullet flew,

And sudden anguish seiz'd the silent ewe ;

Stagg'ring, she falls upon the verdant plain,

Convulsive pangs distract her wounded brain.

Great PAN beheld her stretch'd upon the grass,

Nor unreveng'd permits the crime to pass :

Th' *Arcadian* God, with grief and fury stung,

Snatch'd his stout crook, and fierce to vengeance sprung ;

His faithful dogs their master's steps pursue :

The fleecy flocks before their father bow.—

With bleatings hoarse salute him as he strode :
And frisking lambkins dance around the God.
The sire of sheep then lifted from the ground
The panting dam, and piss'd upon the wound :
The stream divine soon eas'd the mother's pain ;
The wise immortals never piss in vain.
Then to the ball his horny foot applies,
Before his foot the kick'd offender flies.
The hapless orb a gaping face detain'd ;
Deep sunk in sand the hapless orb remain'd.

  As VERDURILLA mark'd the ball's arrest,
She with resentment fired *Castalio's* breast.
The nymph assum'd *Patrico's* shape and mien,
Like great *Patrico* stalk'd along the green ;
So well his manner and his accent feign'd,
Castalio deemed *Patrico's* self complain'd.
Ah, sad disgrace ! see rustic herds invade
GOLFINIAN plains, the angry fairy said :
Your ball abus'd, your hopes and projects cross'd,
The game endanger'd, and the hole nigh lost.
Thus brutal PAN resents his wounded ewe,
Tho' chance, not you, did guide the fatal blow.

Incens'd *Castalio* makes her no replies,
T' attack the God, the furious mortal flies :
His iron-headed club around he swings, .
And fierce at PAN the pond'rous weapon flings.
Affrighted PAN the dreadful missive shunn'd,
But blameless *Tray* receiv'd a deadly wound :
Ill-fated *Tray* no more the flocks shall tend,
In anguish doom'd his shorten'd life to end.
Nor could great PAN afford a timely aid ;
Great PAN himself before the hero fled :
Even he—a God—a mortal's fury dreads,
And far and fast from bold *Castalio* speeds.

To free the ball the chief now turns his mind,
Flies to the bank where lay the orb confined ;
The pond'rous club upon the ball descends.
Involv'd in dust th' exulting orb ascends.
Their loud applause the pleas'd spectators raise ;
The hollow bank resounds *Castalio's* praise.

A mighty blow *Pygmalion* then lets fall,
Straight from th' impulsive engine starts the ball,
Answ'ring its master's just design, it hastes,
And from the hole scarce twice two clubs' length rests.

Ah ! what avails thy skill, since fate decrees
Thy conqu'ring foe to bear away the prize !
  Full fifteen clubs' length from the hole he lay
A wide cart-road before him cross'd his way ;
The deep-cut tracks th' intrepid chief defies ;
High o'er the road the ball triumphing flies,
Lights on the green, and scours into the hole ;
Down with it sinks depress'd *Pygmalion's* soul.
Seiz'd with surprise, th' affrighted hero stands,
And feebly tips the ball with trembling hands.
The creeping ball its want of force complains,
A grassy tuft the loit'ring orb detains.
Surrounding crowds the victor's praise proclaim,
The echoing shore resounds *Castalio's* name.
  For him *Pygmalion* must the bowl prepare.
To him must yield the honours of the war ;
On fame's triumphant wings his name shall soar
Till time shall end, or GOFFING be no more.

ADDRESS TO ST. ANDREWS.

St. Andrews! they say that thy glories are gone,
That thy streets are deserted, thy castles o'erthrown :
If thy glories *be* gone, they are only, methinks,
As it were, by enchantment, transferr'd to thy Links.
Though thy streets be not now, as of yore, full of prelates,
Of abbots and monks, and of hot-headed zealots,
Let none judge us rashly, or blame us as scoffers,
When we say that instead there are Links full of Goffers,
With more of good heart and good feeling among them
Than the abbots, the monks, or the zealots who sung them :
We have red coats and bonnets, we've putters and clubs ;
The green has its bunkers, its hazards, and *rubs ;*
At the long hole across we have biscuits and beer,
And the Hebes who sell it give zest to the cheer :
If this make not up for the pomp and the splendour
Of mitres, and murders, and mass—we'll surrender :

If Goffers and caddies be not better neighbours
Than abbots and soldiers, with crosses and sabres,
Let such fancies remain with the fool who so thinks,
While we toast old St. Andrews, its Goffers and Links.

THE GOLFIAD.

Arma, virumq. cano.—Virgil, *Æn.* i. l. i.

Balls, clubs, and men I sing, who first, methinks,
Made sport and bustle on North Berwick Links,
Brought coin and fashion, betting, and renown,
Champagne and claret, to a country town,
And lords and ladies, knights and squires, to ground
Where washerwomen erst and snobs were found !

Had I the powers of him who sung of Troy—
Gem of the learned, bore of every boy—
Or him, the bard of Rome, who, later, told
How great Æneas roam'd and fought of old—
I then might shake the gazing world like them ;
For who denies I have as grand a theme ?
Time-honour'd Golf !—I heard it whisper'd once
That he who could not play was held a dunce

On old Olympus, when it teem'd with gods.

O rare!—but it's a lie—I'll bet the odds!

No doubt these heathen gods, the very minute

They knew the game, would have delighted in it!

Wars, storms, and thunders—all would have been off!

Mars, Jove, and Neptune would have studied Golf,

And swiped—like Oliphant and Wood below—

Smack over hell* at one immortal go!

Had Mecca's Prophet known the noble game

Before he gave his paradise to fame,

He would have promis'd, in the land of light,

Golf all the day—and Houris all the night!

But this is speculation : we must come,

And work the subject rather nearer home :

Lest, in attempting all too high to soar,

We fall, like Icarus, to rise no more.

•

   The game is ancient—manly—and employs.

In its departments, women, men, and boys :

---

* Hell is a range of broken ground on St. Andrews Links,
bearing probably the same proportion to the *ordinary* course of the
Links as hell would to heaven in the opinion of these immortals.

Men play the game, the boys the clubs convey,
And lovely woman gives the prize away,
When August brings the great, the medal day!
Nay, more : tho' some may doubt, and sneer, and scoff,
The female muse has sung the game of Goff,
And trac'd it down, with choicest skill and grace,
Thro' all its bearings, to the human race ;
The tee, the start of youth—the game, our life—
The ball when fairly bunkered, man and wife.

Now, Muse, assist me while I strive to name
The varied skill and chances of the game.
Suppose we play a match : if all agree,
Let Clan and Saddell tackle Baird and me.
Reader, attend ! and learn to play at Goff ;
The lord of Saddell and myself strike off !
He strikes—he's in the ditch—this hole is ours ;
Bang goes my ball—it's bunker'd, by the pow'rs.
But better play succeeds, these blunders past,
And in six strokes the hole is halved at last.

O hole ! tho' small, and scarcely to be seen,
Till we are close upon thee, on the green :

And tho' when seen, save Golfers, few can prize.

The value, the delight that in thee lies :

Yet, without thee, our tools were useless all—

The club, the spoon, the putter, and the ball :

For all is done—each ball arranged on tee,

Each stroke directed—but to enter thee !

If—as each tree, and rock, and cave of old,

Had *its* presiding nymph, as we are told—

Thou hast *thy* nymph : I ask for nothing but

Her aid propitious when I come to putt.

Now for the second : And here Baird and Clan

In turn must prove which is the better man :

Sir David swipes sublime !—into the quarry !*

Whiz goes the chief—a sneezer,† by Old Harry !

" Now, lift the stones, but do not touch the ball.

The hole is lost if it but move at all :

Well play'd, my cock ! you could not have done more :

'Tis bad, but still we may get home at four."

* A place on North Berwick Links, so awkward, that in playing
out of it one is allowed to remove everything, provided the position
of the ball is not altered.

† A long and scientific stroke at golf.

E

Now, near the hole Sir David plays the odds ;
Clan plays the like, and wins it, by the gods !
" A most disgusting *steal;** well, come away,
They're one ahead, but we have four to play.
We'll win it yet, if I can cross the ditch :
They're over, smack ! come, there's another *sich.*" †
Baird plays a trump—we hole at three—they stare,
And miss their putt—so now the match is square.

And here, who knows but, as old Homer sung,
The scales of fight on Jove's own finger hung ?
Here Clan and Saddell : there swing Baird and I.—
Our merits, that's to say ; for half an eye
Could tell, if *bodies* in the scales were laid,
Which must descend, and which must rise ahead.

If Jove were thus engaged, we did not see him,
But told our boys to clean the balls and tee 'em.
In this next hole the turf is most uneven :
We play like tailors—only in at seven,

* *Steal,* the act of holing the ball contrary to probability.
† A slang term for *sich.*

And they at six; most miserable play!

But let them laugh who win.   Hear Saddell say,

" Now, by the piper who the pibroch played

Before old Moses, we are one ahead,

And only two to play—a special *coup.'*

Three five-pound notes to one !" " Done, sir, with you."

We start again; and in this dangerous hole *

Full many a stroke is played with heart and soul :

" Give me the iron !" either party cries,

As in the quarry, track, or sand he lies.

We reach the green at last, at even strokes :

Some caddy chatters, *that* the chief provokes,

And makes him miss his putt; Baird holes the ball :

Thus, with but one to play, 'tis even all !

'Tis strange, and yet there cannot be a doubt,

That such a snob should put a chieftain out :

The noble lion, thus, in all his pride,

Stung by the gadfly, roars and starts aside ;

Clan did *not* roar—*he* never makes a noise—

But said, " They're very troublesome, these boys."

Fifth hole.

His partner muttered something not so civil,

Particularly, " scoundrels "—" at the devil !"

Now Baird and Clan in turn strike off and play *

Two strokes, the best that have been seen to-day.

His spoon next Saddell takes, and plays a trump—

Mine should have been as good but for a bump

That turn'd it off.   Baird plays the odds—it's all

But in !—at five yards, good, Clan holes the ball !

My partner, self, and song—all three are done !

We lose the match, and all the bets thereon !

Perhaps you think that, tho' I'm not a winner.

My muse should stay and celebrate the dinner ;

The ample joints that travel up the stair.

To grace the table spread by Mrs. Blair ;

The wine, the ale, the toasts, the jokes, the songs.

And all that to such revelry belongs ;—

It may not be ! 'twere fearful falling off

To sing such trifles after singing Golf

In most majestic strain : let others dwell

On such, and rack their carnal brains to tell

A tale of sensuality !—Farewell !

* Sixth hole.

THE FIRST HOLE AT ST. ANDREWS
ON A CROWDED DAY.

Forsan et hæc olim meminisse juvabit.—ÆN. i. l. 208.

'Tis morn ! and man awakes, by sleep refresh'd.

To do whate'er he has to do with zest :

But at St. Andrews, where my scene is laid,

One only thought can enter every head :

The thought of Golf, to wit—and that engages

Men of all sizes, tempers, ranks, and ages :

The root—the *primum mobile* of all,

The epidemic of the club and ball :

The work by day, the source of dreams by night,

The never-failing fountain of delight !

Here, Mr. Philp, club-maker, is as great

As Philip—as any minister of state !

And every caddy as profess'd a hero

As Captain Cook, or Wellington, or Nero !

For instance—Davie, oldest of the cads,

Who gives *half-one* to unsuspicious lads,

When he *might* give them *two*, or even *more*,

And win, perhaps, three matches out of four,

Is just as politic in *his* affairs

As Talleyrand or Metternich in *theirs*.

He has the statesman's elements, 'tis plain,

Cheat, flatter, humbug—*anything* for gain ;

And had he trod the world's wide field, methinks,

As long as he has trod St. Andrews Links,

He might have been prime minister, or priest,

My lord, or plain *Sir David* at the least !

Now, to the ground of Golf my muse shall fly,

The various men assembled to descry,

Nine-tenths of whom, throughout the rolling year,

At the first hole *unfailingly* appear ;

Where, "How d'ye do ?" "Fine morning," "Rainy day,"

And, "What's the match ?" are preludes to the play.

So full the meeting that I scarcely can,

In such a crowd, distinguish man from man.

We'll take them as they come :—He next the wall,

Outside, upon the right, is Mr. Saddell ;

And well he plays, though, rising on his toes,

Whiz round his head his *supple* club he throws.

There, Doctor Moodie, turtle-like, displays

His well-filled paunch, and swipes beyond all praise :

While Cuttlehill, of slang and chatter chief,

Provokes the bile of Captain George Moncrieffe.

See Colonel Playfair, shaped in form *rotund*,

Parade, the unrivall'd Falstaff of the ground ;

He laughs and jokes, plays, "what you like," and yet

You'll rarely find him make a foolish bet.

Against the sky, display'd in high relief.

I see the figure of Clanranald's Chief,

Dress'd most correctly in the *fancy* style,

Well-whisker'd face, and radiant with a smile :

He bows, shakes hands, and has a word for all—

So did Beau Nash, as master of the ball !

Near him is Saddell, dress'd in blue coat plain,

With lots of Gourlays,* free from spot or stain :

---

* Meaning plenty of balls, made by Mr. Gourlay of Bruntsfield Links, a famous artist. The gentleman alluded to generally has, at *least*, twelve dozen.

He whirls his club to catch the proper *swing,*

And freely bets round all the scarlet ring ;

And swears by *Ammon,* he'll engage to drive

As long a ball as any man alive !

That's Major Playfair, a man of nerve unshaken—

He knows a thing or two, or I'm mistaken ;

And when he's press'd, can play a tearing game.

He works for *certainty* and not for *Fame!*

There's none—I'll back the assertion with a wager—

Can play the *heavy iron* like the Major.

Next him is Craigie Halkett, one who can

Swipe out, for distance, against any man ;

But in what *course* the ball so struck may go,

No looker on—not he himself—can know.

See Major Holcroft, he's a steady hand

Among the best of all the Golfing band ;

He plays a winning game in every part,

But near the hole displays the greatest art.

There young Patullo stands, and he, methinks,

Can drive the longest ball upon the Links ;

And well he plays the spoon and iron, but

He fails a *little* when he comes to *putt.*

Near Captain Cheape, a sailor by profession

(But not so good at Golf as navigation),

Is Mr. Peter Glass, who once could play

A better game than he can do to-day.

We cannot last for ever ! and the *gout*,

Confirmed, is wondrous apt to put us out.

There, to the left, I see Mount-Melville stand

Erect, his *driving putter* in his hand ;

It is a club he cannot leave behind,

It works the balls so well against the wind.

Sir David Erskine has come into play,

He has not won the medal *yet*, but *may*.

Dost love the greatest laugher of the lot ?—

Then play a round with little Mr. Scott :

He is a merry cock, and seems to me

To win or lose with equal ecstasy.

Here's Mr. Messieux, he's a noble player,

But something *nervous*—that's a bad affair ;

It sadly spoils his putting, when he's *press'd*—

But let him *win*, and he will beat the *best*.

That little man that's seated on the ground

In red, must be Carnegie, I'll be bound !

A most conceited dog, not slow to *go it*

At Golf, or anything—a *sort* of poet ;

He talks to Wood—John Wood—who ranks among

The tip-top hands that to the Club belong ;

And Oliphant, the rival of the last,

Whose play, at times, can scarcely be surpass'd.

Who's he that's just arrived ?—I know him well :

It is the Cupar Provost, John Dalzell :

When he *does* hit the ball, he swipes like blazes—

It is but *seldom*, and *himself* amazes ;

But when he winds his horn, and leads the chase,

The Laird of Lingo's in his proper place.

It has been *said* that, at the *break of day*

His Golf is better than his evening play :

That must be scandal ; for I am sure that none

Could think of Golf before the rise of sun.

He now is talking to his lady's brother,

A man of politics, Sir Ralph Anstruther :

Were he but once in Parliament, methinks,

And working *there* as well as on the *Links*,

The burghs, I'll be bound, would not repent them

That they had such a man to represent them :

There's *one thing* only—when he's *on the roll*,
He must not lose his *nerve*, as when he's near the hole.
Upon his right is Major Bob Anstruther :
Cobbet's *one* radical—and he's *another*.

But when we meet, as here, to play at Golf,
Whig, Radical, and Tory—all are off—
Off the contested politics, I mean—
And fun and harmony illume the scene.
We make our matches from the love of playing,
Without one loathsome feeling but the *paying*,
And that is lessened by the thought, we *borrow*
Only to-day what we shall *win* to-morrow.
Then, here's prosperity to Golf ! and long
May those who play be cheerful, fresh, and strong :
When *driving* ceases, may we still be able
To play the *shorts, putt,* and be comfortable !
And to the latest may we fondly cherish
The thoughts of Golf—so let St. Andrews flourish !

ANOTHER PEEP AT THE LINKS.

Alter erit tum Typhys, et altera quæ vehat Argo
Dilectos heroas—erunt etiam altera bella.

VIRG. GEORGIC.

AWAKE, my slumb'ring Muse, and plume thy wing,
Our former theme—the Game of Golf—to sing !
For since the subject last inspired my pen,
Ten years have glided by, or nearly ten.
Still the old hands at Golf delight to play—
Still new succeed them as they pass away ;
Still ginger-beer and parliament are seen
Serv'd out by Houris to the peopled green ;
And still the royal game maintains its place,
And will maintain it through each rising race.

    Still Major Playfair shines, a star at Golf ;
And still the Colonel—though a *little* off ;

The former, skill'd in many a curious art,

As chemist, mechanist, can play his part,

And understands, besides the pow'r of swiping,

Electro-Talbot-and Daguerreotyping.

Still Colonel Holcroft steady walks the grass,

And still his putting nothing can surpass—

And still he drives, unless the weather's rough,

Not quite so far as *once*, but far enough.

Still Saddell walks, superb, improved in play,

Though his blue jacket now is turn'd to grey ;

Still are his balls as rife and clean as wont—

Still swears by Ammon, and still bets the *blunt*—

Still plays all matches—still is often beat—

And still in iced punch drowns each fresh defeat.

Still on the green Clanranald's chief appears,

As gay as ever, as untouch'd by years ;

He laughs at Time, and Time, perhaps through whim,

Respects his nonchalance, and laughs at him ;

Just fans him with his wings, but spares his head,

As loth to lose a subject so well bred.

Sir Ralph returns—he has been absent long—
No less renown'd in Golfing than in song ;
With continental learning richly stored,
Teutonic Bards translated and explored ;
A *litéraire*—a German scholar now,
With all *Griselda's* honours on his brow !

The Links have still the pleasure to behold
Messieux, complete in matches, as of old ;
He, modest, tells you that his day's gone by :
If any think it *is so*—let them try !
Still portly William Wood is to be seen,
As good as ever on the velvet green,
The same unfailing trump ; but John, methinks,
Has taken to the *Turf*, and shies the Links.

Whether the *Leger* and the *Derby* pay
As well as *Hope Grant*, I can scarcely say ;
But let that be—'tis better, John, old fellow,
To pluck the *rooks*, than *rook* the *violoncello*.

Permit me just a moment to digress—
Friendship would chide me should I venture less—

The poor Chinese, there cannot be a doubt,
Will shortly be demolish'd out and out ;
But—O how blest beyond the common line
Of conquer'd nations by the Power divine !—
Saltoun to cut their yellow throats, and then
Hope Grant to play their requiem-notes—Amen !

Still George Moncrieffe appears the crowd before,
Lieutenant-Colonel—Captain now no more ;
Improv'd in ev'rything—in looks and life,
And, more than all, the husband of a wife !

As in the olden time, see Craigie Halkett—
Wild strokes and swiping, jest, and fun, and rackett :
He leaves us now.   But in three years, I trust.
He will return, and sport his *muzzle dust*,
Play Golf again, and patronise all cheer.
From noble *Claret* down to *bitter beer*.

Mount-Melville still erect as ever stands,
And plies his club with energetic hands,
Plays short and steady, often is a winner—
A better Captain never graced a dinner.

But where is *Oliphant,* that artist grand ?
He scarce appears among the Golfing band.
No doubt he's married ; but when that befalls
Is there an end to putters, clubs, and balls ?
Not so, methinks : *Sir David Baird* can play
With any Golfer of the present day ;
The *Laird of Lingo,* Major Bob Anstruther—
Both married, and the one as good's the other.

Dalgleish and Haig, two better men to play
You scarce will meet upon a summer's day ;
Alike correct, whatever may befall,
Swipe, iron, putter, quarter-stroke, and all.

Old Robert Lindsay plays a decent game,
Tho' not a Golfer of *enormous* fame.
Well can he fish with minnow as with fly,
Paint, and play *farthing-brag* uncommonly ;
Give jolly dinners, justice courts attend—
A good companion and a steady friend.

But *Cuttlehill,* that wonderful *buffoon,*
We meet him now no more, as wont, at noon ;

No more along the green his jokes are heard,
And some who *dared* not *then*, now take the word.
Farewell! facetious Jem—too surely gone—
A loss to us—*Joe Miller* to *Boulogne*.

Poor Peter Glass, a worthy soul and *blue*,
Has paid the debt of nature—'tis too true!
Long did his candle flicker with the gout—
One puff, a little stronger, *blew it out*.
And good Patullo! he who drove as none,
Since him, have driven—he is also gone!
And Captain Cheape—who does not mourn the day
That snatch'd so good, so kind a friend away?
One more I name—and only one—but he
Was older far, and lower in degree—
Great Davie Robertson, the eldest cad,
In whom the good was stronger than the bad;
He sleeps in death! and with him sleeps a skill
Which Davie, statesmanlike, could wield at will!
Sound be his slumbers! yet if he should wake
In worlds where Golf is play'd, himself he'd shake,
And look about, and tell each young beginner,

" I'll gie half-ane—nae mair, as I'm a sinner."

He leaves a son, and Allan is his name,

In Golfing far beyond his father's fame ;

Tho' in diplomacy, I shrewdly guess,

His skill's inferior, and his fame is less.

Now for the *mushrooms*—old, perchance, or new—

But whom my former strain did not review :

I'll name an *old one*, Patton, Tom, of Perth,

Short, stout, grey-headed, but of sterling worth !

A Golfer perfect—something, it may be,

The worse for *wear*, but few so true as he ;

Good-humour'd when behind as when ahead,

And drinks like blazes till he goes to bed.

His friend is Peddie, not an awful swiper,

But at the putting he's a very *viper* :

Give him a man to drive him through the green,

And he'll be bad to beat, it will be seen—

Patton and Peddie—Peddie and Patton,

Are just the people one should bet upon.

There Keith with Andrew Wauchope works away,

And most respectable the game they play :

The navy Captain's steadiness and age
Give him, perhaps, the *pull*—but I'll engage,
Ere some few months, or rather weeks, are fled,
Youth and activity will take the lead.

See Gilmour next—and he can drive a ball
As far as any man among them all ;
In ev'ry hunting-field can lead the van,
And is throughout a perfect gentleman.

Next comes a handsome man, with Roman nose
And whiskers dark—Wolfe Murray I suppose ;
He has begun but lately, still he plays
A fairish game, and therefore merits praise :
Ask him when at his *worst*, and he will say,
" 'Tis bad—but, Lord ! how I play'd *yesterday !*"

Another man with whiskers—stout and strong—
A Golfer too who swipes his balls along,
And well he putts, but I should simply say,
His *own opinion's* better than his play ;
Dundas can sing a song, or glee, or catch,
I think far better than he makes a match.

But who is he whose hairy lips betray
Hussar or Lancer?   Muse, oh kindly say !
'Tis Captain Feilden.   Lord, how hard he hits !
'Tis strange he does not knock the ball to bits !
Sometimes he hits it fair, and makes a stroke
Whose distance Saddell's envy might provoke ;
But take his *common* play ; the worst that ever
Play'd Golf might give him *one*, and beat him clever.
Bad tho' he be, the Captain has done more
Than ever man who play'd at Golf before :
One thund'ring ball he drove—'twas in despair—
Wide of the hole, indeed, but kill'd a *hare !*

Ah ! Captain Campbell, old Schehallion, see !
Most have play'd longer, few so well as he ;—
A sterling Highlander, and that's no trifle,—
So thinks the *Gael*—a workman with a rifle ;
Keeps open house—a very proper thing—
And, tho' rheumatic, *fiddles* like a king !

Sir Thomas of Moncrieffe—I cannot doubt
But he will be a Golfer out and out :

Tho' now, perhaps, he's off, and careless too—
His misses numerous, his hits are few;
But he is zealous; and the time will be
When few will better play the game than he.
Balbirnie and Makgill will both be good—
Strong, active, lathy fellows; so they should.

But for John Grant, a clever fellow too,
I really fear that Golf will never do.
'Tis strange, indeed; for he can paint, and ride,
And hunt the hounds, and many a thing beside;
Amuse his friends with anecdote and fun;
But when he takes his club in hand—he's *done!*
Stay! I retract!—Since writing the above,
I've seen him play a better game, by Jove;
So much beyond what one could have believ'd,
That I confess myself for once deceived;
And if he can go on the season through,
There's still a *chance* that he may really *do*.

I've kept a man, in *petto*, for the last—
Not an old Golfer, but by few surpassed—

Great Captain Fairlie !   When he drives a ball—
One of his *best*—for he don't hit them all,
It then requires no common stretch of sight
To watch its progress, and to see it light.

One moment : I've another to define—
A famous sportsman, and a judge of wine—
Whom faithful Mem'ry offers to my view ;
He made the game a study, it is true ;
Still, many play as well but, for *position*
John Buckle fairly beggars competition !

And now farewell !   I am the worse for wear—
Grey is my jacket, growing grey my hair !
And though my play is pretty much the same.
Mine is, at best, a despicable game.
But still I like it—still delight to sing
Clubs, players, caddies, balls, and everything.
But all that's bright must fade, and we who play,
Like those before us, soon must pass away :
Yet it requires no prophet's skill to trace
The royal game thro' each succeeding race :

While on the tide of generations flows,
It still shall bloom, a never-fading rose ;
And still St. Andrews Links, with flags unfurl'd,
Shall peerless reign, and challenge all the world !

THE NINE HOLES OF THE LINKS OF ST. ANDREWS.

IN A SERIES OF SONNETS.

>>◆◆◆<

I. THE FIRST OR BRIDGE HOLE.

SACRED to hope and promise is the spot--
    To Philp's and to the Union Parlour near.
    To every Golfer, every caddie dear-
Where we strike off—oh, ne'er to be forgot.
Although in lands most distant we sojourn.
    But not without its perils is the place :
    Mark the opposing caddie's sly grimace.
Whispering : " He's on the road !" " He's in the burn !"
So is it often in the grander game
    Of life, when, eager, hoping for the palm,

Breathing of honour, joy, and love and fame,

    Conscious of nothing like a doubt or qualm,

We start, and cry : "Salute us, muse of fire !"

    And the first footstep lands us in the mire.

                          R. C.

II. THE SECOND OR CARTGATE HOLE.

FEARFUL to Tyro is thy primal stroke,

    O Cartgate ! for behold the bunker opes

    Right to the *teeing*-place its yawning chops,

Hope to engulf ere it is well awoke.

That passed, a Scylla in the form of rushes

    Nods to Charybdis which in ruts appears :

    He will be safe who in the middle steers ;

One step aside, the ball destruction brushes.

Golf symbols thus again our painful life,

    Dangers in front, and pitfalls on each hand :

    But see, one glorious cleek-stroke from the sand

Sends Tyro home, and saves all further strife !

He's in at six—old Sandy views the lad

With new respect, remarking : " That's no bad !"

                          R. C.

III. THE THIRD HOLE.

No rest in Golf—still perils in the path :
　　Here, playing a good ball, perhaps it goes
　　Gently into the *Principalian Nose*,
Or else *Tam's Coo*, which equally is death.
Perhaps the wind will catch it in mid-air,
　　And take it to *the Whins*—" Look out, look out !
　　Tom Morris, be. oh be. a faithful scout !"
But Tom, though *links-eyed*, finds not anywhere.
Such thy mishaps, O Merit : feeble balls
　　Meanwhile roll on, and lie upon the green ;
'Tis well. my friends, if you, when this befalls,
　　Can spare yourselves the infamy of spleen.
It only shows the ancient proverb's force,
That you may further go and fare the worse.

　　　　　　　　　　　　　　　　　R. C.

IV. THE FOURTH OR GINGER-BEER HOLE.

THOUGH thou hast lost this last unlucky hole,
　　I say again. betake thee not to swearing.
　　Or any form of speech profanely daring.
Though some allege it tendeth to console

Better do thou thy swelling griefs control,

    Sagacious that at hand a joy awaits thee

    (Since out of doubt a glass of beer elates thee),

Without that frightful peril to thy soul.

A glass of beer! go dip thine angry beak in it,

    And straight its rage will melt to soft placidity,

That solace finding thou art wise to seek in it :

    Ah, do not thou on this poor plea reject it,

That in thy inwards it will breed acidity—

One glass of Stewart's brandy will correct it.

                      P. A.

V. THE HELL HOLE.

WHAT daring genius first yclept thee Hell !

    What high, poetic, awe-struck grand old Golfer.

    Much more of a mythologist than scoffer !

Whoe'er he was, the name befits thee well.

" All hope abandon, ye who enter here,"

    Is written awful o'er thy gloomy jaws,

    A threat to all save Allan might give pause :

And frequent from within come tones of fear-

Dread sound of cleeks, which ever fall in vain.

And—for mere mortal patience is but scanty—

Shriekings thereafter, as of souls in pain,

    Dire gnashings of the teeth, and horrid curses.

    With which I need not decorate my verses.

Because, in fact, you'll find them all in Dante.

                              P. A.

VI. THE HEATHER HOLE.

Ah me ! prodigious woes do still environ—

    To quote verbatim from some grave old poet—

The man who needs must meddle with his *iron ;*

    And here, if ever, thou art doomed to know it.

For now behold thee, doubtless for thy sins,

    Tilling some bunker, as if on a lease of it,

    And so assiduous to make due increase of it :

Or wandering homeless through a world of whins !

And when, these perils past, thou seemest *dead*,

    And hop'st a half—O woe, the ball goes crooked.

Making thy foe just one more hole ahead,

    Surely a consummation all too sad.

Without that sneering devilish " Never lookit,"

    The parting comment of the opposing cad.

                              P. A.

VII. THE HIGH OR EDEN HOLE.

THE shelly pit is cleared at one fell blow,

    A stroke to be remembered in your dreams !

    But here the Eden on your vision gleams,

Lovely, but treach'rous in its solemn flow.

The hole is perched aloft, too near the tide,

    The green is small, and broken is the ground

    Which doth that little charmed space surround !

Go not too far, and go not to a side ;

Take the short spoon to do your second stroke ;

    Sandy entreats you will the wind take heed on,

For, oh, it would a very saint provoke,

    If you should let your ball plump in the Eden.

You do your best, but who can fate control ?

So here against you is another hole.

R. C. Jr.

VIII. THE SHORT HOLE.

BRIEF but not easy is the next adventure ;

    Legend avers it has been done in *one*,

    Though such long *steals* are now but rarely done—

In *three* 'twere well that you the hole should enter.

Strangely original is this bit of ground,
    For, while at hand the smooth and smiling green,
    One bunker wide and bushy yawns between,
Where Tyro's gutta is too often found.
Nervous your rival strikes and heels his ball—
    From that whin-bush at six he'll scarce extract it :
    Yours, by no blunder this time counteracted,
Is with the grass-club lofted over all.
There goes a hole in your side—how you hug it !
Much as th' Australian digger does a nugget.

                                                R. C. Jr.

IX. THE END HOLE.

THE end, but not the end—the distance-post
    That halves the game—a serious point to thee,
    For if one more thou losest. 'twill be *three :*
Yet even in that case, think not all is lost.
Men four behind have been, on the return.
    So favoured by Olympus, or by care,
    That all their terrors vanished into air,
And caddies cried them *dormy* at the burn !

I could quote proverbs, did I speak at random :

　　Full many a broken ship comes into port,

　　Full many a cause is gained at last resort,

But Golf impresses most, *Nil desperandum.*

Turn, then, my son, with two against, nor dread

To gain the winning-post with one ahead.

R. C. Jr.

The following SCRAP relative to GOLF occurs in a very rare work entitled *Westminster Drollery*, 12mo, 1671, p. 28.

A Song called—

"And to each pretty lass

We will give a green gown."

THUS all our life long we are frolick and gay,

And instead of Court revels we merrily play

At Trap, at Rules, and at Barly-break run,

At GOFF and at Foot-Ball; and when we have done

These innocent sports, we'll laugh and lie down,

And to each pretty lass

We will give a green gown.

N.B.— The above was copied from a book containing many curious Scraps relating to Golfing, Archery, and Curling, belonging to JAMES MAIDMENT, Esq., advocate.

THE GOLFER'S GARLAND. *

Of rural diversions, too long has the chase
All the honours usurped, and assumed the chief place ;
But truth bids the muse from henceforward proclaim,
That Golfing of field sports stands foremost in fame.

> With a fal-the-ral-a, etc.

At Golf we contend without rancour or spleen,
And bloodless the laurels we reap on the green ;
From vig'rous exertions our pleasures arise,
And to crown our delight no poor fugitive dies.

> With a fal-the-ral-a, etc.

----

* From Mathieson's Poem "The Goff" 1743. with the ex-
ception of the 5th verse, which was copied by a member of the
Burgess Club from a version of the song found on an old bookstall.

O'er the green see our heroes in uniform clad,

In parties well matched how they gracefully spread,

Whilst with long strokes, and short strokes, they tend
to the goal,

And with putt well directed plump into the hole.

With a fal-the-ral-a, etc.

From exercise keen, from strength active and bold.

We traverse the green, and forget to grow old ;

Blue devils, diseases, dull sorrow and care,

Are knock'd down by our balls as they whiz through the air.

With a fal-the-ral-a, etc.

The strong-sinew'd son of Alcmena would drub,

And demolish a monster when armed with a club ;

But what were the monsters which Hercules slew,

To those fiends which each week with our balls we subdue ?

With a fal-the-ral-a, etc.

Health, happiness, harmony, friendship, and fame,

Are the fruits and rewards of our favourite game :

A sport so distinguished the fair must approve ;

So to Golf give the day and the evening to love.

With a fal the-ral a, etc.

Our first standing toast we to Golfing assign,

No other amusement so truly divine ;

It has charms for the aged, as well as the young.

Then as first of field sports let its praises be sung.

        With a fal-the-ral-a, etc.

And to crown our devotion, and grateful goodwill,

A bumper brimhigh to their healths let us fill ;

Our charming instructresses—blessings attend them,

And cursed be the clown who would dare to offend them !

        With a fal-the-ral-a, etc.

The next we shall drink to our friends far and near :

To the mem'ry of those who no longer appear,

Who have play'd their last round, and passed over that bourne

From which the best Golfer can never return.

        With a fal-the-ral-a, etc.

Then fill up your glass, and let each social soul

Drink to the putter, the balls, and the hole ;

And may every true Golfer invariably find

His opponent play fair, and his fair one prove kind.

        With a fal-the ral-a, etc.

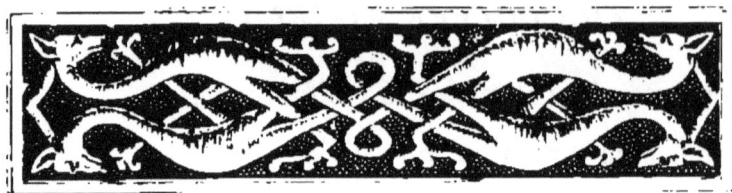

THE LINKS O' INNERLEVEN.

Sung at the Autumn Meeting of the Innerleven
Golfing Club, 1841.

Tune— Dainty Davie.

Wha wad be free from doctor's bills—
From trash o' powders and o' pills—
Will find a cure for a' his ills
    On the Links o' Innerleven.
For there whar lassies bleach their claes,
And bairnies toddle doun the braes,
The merry Golfer daily plays
    On the Links o' Innerleven.

Sae hie ye to the Golfer's ha',
And there, arranged alang the wa',
O' presses ye will see a raw,
    At the Club o' Innerleven.

There from some friendly box ye'll draw
A club and second-handed ba',—
A Gourlay pill's the best o' a'
    For health at Innerleven.

And though the Golfer's sport be keen,
Yet oft upon the putting-green
He'll rest to gaze upon the scene
    That lies round Innerleven—
To trace the steamboat's crumpled way
Through Largo's loch-like silvery bay,
Or to hear the hushing breakers play
    On the beach o' Innerleven.

When in the evening of my days,
I wish I could a cottage raise
Beneath the snugly-sheltering braes
    O'erhanging Innerleven.
There in the plot before the door
I'd raise my vegetable store,
Or tug for supper at the oar
    In the bay near Innerleven.

But daily on thy matchless ground
I and my caddie would be found,
Describing still another round
    On thy Links, sweet Innerleven !
Would I care then for fortune's rubs,
And a' their Kirk and State hubbubs,
While I could stump and swing my clubs
    On the Links o' Innerleven ?

And when the e'ening grey sat doun.
I'd cast aside my tacket* shoon,
And crack o' putter, cleek, and spoon,†
    Wi' a friend at Innerleven.
Syne o'er a glass o' Cameron Brig,‡
A nightcap we would doucely swig,
Laughing at Conservative and Whig,
    By the Links o' Innerleven.

---

  * Golfers wear tacks in their shoes that they may stand firm when they strike.

  † Names for different kinds of clubs.

  ‡ The name of a noted distillery.

IN PRAISE OF *GUTTA PERCHA*.

(1856.)

Of a' the changes that of late
Have shaken Europe's social state—
Let wondering politicians prate,
  And 'bout them mak a wark a'—
A subject mair congenial here,
And dearer to a Golfer's ear
I sing—the change brought round last year
  By balls of *Gutta Percha !*

Tho' Gouf be of our games most rare,
Yet truth to speak, the tear and wear
O' balls was felt to be severe,
  And source o' great vexation :

When Gourlay's balls cost half-a-croun,
And Allan's no a farthing doun,
The feck o's wad been harried soon,
    In this era of taxation.

But times are changed—we dinna care
Though we may ne'er drive leather mair.
Be't stuffed wi' feather or wi' hair—
    For noo we're independent.
At last a substance we hae got,
Frae which for scarce mair than a groat,
A ba' comes that can row and stot—
    A ba' the most transcendent.

Hail, *Gutta Percha*, precious gum !
O'er Scotland's links lang may ye bum :
Some purse-proud billies haw and hum,
    And say ye're douf at fleein' :
But let them try ye fairly out,
Wi' ony balls for days about,
Your merits they will loudly tout,
    And own they hae been leein'.

And noo that a' your praise is spent,
Ye'll listen to a friend's comment,
And kindlier tak on wi' paint,
    Then ye wad be perfection,
And sure some scientific loon,
On Golfing will bestow a boon,
And gie ye a cosmetic soon,
    And brighten your complexion.

"FAR AND SURE!"

By the late Sheriff Logan.

"Far and sure! far and sure!" 'twas the cry of our fathers,
  'Twas a cry which their forefathers heard ;
'Tis the cry of their sons when the mustering gathers :
  When we're gone may it still be the word.

"Far and sure!" there is honour and hope in the sound :
  Long over these Links may it roll !
It will— O it will ! for each face around
  Shows its magic is felt in each soul.

Let it guide us in life : at the desk or the bar.
  It will shield us from folly's gay lure ;
Then, tho' rough be the course, and the winning post *far*,
  We will carry the stakes— O be *sure!*

Let it guide us in Golf, whether " Burgess" or " Star:"
  At the last round let none look demure :
All Golfers are brothers when *driving* is *far*.
  When putting is canny and *sure*.

" Far and sure! far and sure!" fill the bumper and drain it.
  May our motto for ever endure :
May time never maim it, nor dishonour stain it ;
  Then drink, brothers, drink, " Far and sure !"

SONG.

Text — *Scotland yet.*

Gae bring my guid auld clubs ance mair—
 Come, laddie, bring them fast,
For I maun hae anither game,
 E'er the autumn season's past :
And trow ye as I play, my lads,
 My song shall ever be,
" Auld Scotland's royal game o' Gouf
 Our country's game for me."
 Then here's a toast to Goufin' yet,
 Wi' a' the honours three.

Throw by that walloping surtout
 On wi' my auld red jacket—
Haul aff thae gripless Wellingtons
 For yon shoon wi' mony a tacket.

Hang up that snoring Albert hat—
  Yon foraging-cap for me :
And now a Golfer I walk forth,
  Frae worldly care set free.
    Then here's a toast, etc.

Now, laddie, pouch thae Gourlay ba's,
  Wi' joy they'll dance a reel—
My play-club capers in my hand,
  As supple as an eel.
And see ! my partner's on the green,
  His ba' upon the tee—
Impatient, round he swings his club,
  Making heads o' gowans flee.
    Then here's a toast, etc.

How sweet's the air upon the links
  That stretch along the sea !
Where, bending down white clover heads,
  In silence sips the bee.
Our steps how light ! as on we speed
  O'er bouyant knowes o' balm,

To where our balls in distance lie,

Like mushrooms on the lawn.

Then here's a toast, etc.

And 'tween each stroke how socially

Abreast in crack we go,

And shape o' club and mak o' ba'

Discuss wi' sportsman's glow.

Then hale-lung'd laughter peals aloud.

And banter stingless flies,

And tears o' mirth astonished run

From sad dyspeptics' eyes.

Then here's a toast, etc.

And when some rounds demand a rest,

And appetite is keen,

How sweet to taste the Golfer's fare,

Reclining on the green !

Ne'er aldermen at turtle feast

Washed over with champagne,

Rejoiced like us, as baps we tear,

And jugs o' " Berwick's " drain,

Then here's a toast, etc.

Our caddies at our feet reclined,
    Their sheaves o' clubs at rest—
Happy to hear the Golfers' lore,
    Chew on wi' silent zest.
But up, like giants flushed with wine,
    Again our clubs we wield—
We feel new vigour in our arms,
    And ardent take the field.
        Then here's a toast, etc.

Thus on we've toiled at Dubbieside,
    But 'neath the Lomond hill
The sun has sunk, and the whirling din
    Has ceased at Kirkland Mill.
The sand-eel crowd is thickening black
    By the mouth o' Leven stream,
And the wearied *Tar* in Largo Bay
    Lets off the roaring *steam*.
        So here's a toast, etc.

So here's a health to our ain club,
    St. Andrews next, our mither—

A bumper to Dunbarnie next,

   Our neibour and our brither :

Auld Dubbieside salutes ye a' :

   And if you wish to meet her,

You'll find her ready at a ca',

   Wi' her gallant captain PETER.

      So here's a toast, etc.

A GOLFING SONG.

By Mr. James Ballantine.

Tune—*La Haughty Gaul.*

Come, leave your dingy desks and shops,
 Ye sons of ancient Reekie,
And by green fields and sunny slopes,
 For healthy pastime seek ye.
Don't bounce about your "*dogs of war*,"
 Nor at our *shinties* scoff, boys,
But learn our motto, "*Sure and Far*,"
 Then come and play at Golf, boys.
Chorus—Three rounds of Bruntsfield Links will chase
  All murky vapours off, boys,
  And nothing can your sinews brace
  Like the glorious game of Golf, boys.

Above our head the clear blue sky,
    We bound the gowan'd sward o'er,
And as our balls fly far and high,
    Our bosoms glow with ardour ;
While dear Edina, Scotland's Queen,
    Her misty cap lifts off, boys,
And smiles serenely on the green,
    Graced by the game of Golf, boys.

                    Chorus—Three rounds, etc.

We putt, we drive, we laugh, we chat,
    Our strokes and jokes aye clinking,
We banish all extraneous fat,
    And all extraneous thinking.
We'll cure you of a summer cold,
    Or of a winter cough, boys,
We'll make you young, even when you're old,
    So come and play at Golf, boys.

                    Chorus—Three rounds, etc.

When in the dumps with mulligrubs,
    Or doyte with barley bree, boys,

GOLFING SONG.

Go get you of the green three rubs,
    'Twill set you on the " *Tee*," boys.
There's no disease we cannot cure,
    No care we cannot doff, boys ;
Our aim is ever " *Far and Sure*"—
    So come and play at Golf, boys.
            Chorus—Three rounds, etc.

O blessings on pure cauler air,
    And every healthy sport, boys,
That makes sweet Nature seem more fair.
    And makes long life seem short, boys :
That warms your hearts with genial glow,
    And makes you halve your loaf, boys.
With every needy child of woe—
    So bless the game of Golf, boys.
            Chorus—Three rounds, etc.

Then don your brilliant scarlet coats,
    With your bright blue velvet caps, boys,
And some shall play the *rocket shots*
    And some the *putting paps*, boys.

No son of Scotland, man or boy,

   Shall e'er become an oaf, boys,

Who gathers friendship, health, and joy,

   In playing at the Golf, boys.

             Chorus—Three rounds, etc.

GOLFING SONG.

TUNE — *Clan Pease Strae.*

WHEN Tom and me were laddies,
  Oor pastimes were but sma'—
A game at common shinty,
  Or playin' at the ba' :
But lang since then a game we ken,
  Enticin' great and sma' :
A king I ween aroun' Leith green
  Has often gowff'd the ba'.

Wi' glorious Gowff brave Scotia's game,
  Oor youth comes back ance mair,
When, swift and free as birds on wing,
  Oor balls fly through the air.
The rays o' fortune's golden star
  Most earthly ills can cure :
Gowff helps to keep the others "*far*,"
  Or makes their absence "*sure*."

When ice is keen the curlin' steen
    Wi' birr gaes straught awa',
And cricket on the meadow green,
    Seems manly, brisk, and braw :
But, laddie, tak a club in han',
    Then tee and drive the ba' :
Ye'll find the royal game o' Gowff
    Is better than them a'.

Oor volunteers wi' guns and spears
    Keep foreign foes in awe :
Noo Britain's youth shield north an' south.
    Laigh cot and stately ha' ;
Sae ne'er a foe shall Scotland fear
    While Scotland's game we play,
Though we should leave the *puttin'* green
    To buckle for the fray.

Printed by R. Clark, Edinburgh.

www.ingramcontent.com/pod-product-compliance
Lightning Source LLC
Chambersburg PA
CBHW031452270326
41930CB00007B/966

* 9 7 8 3 3 3 7 0 0 5 6 3 4 *